I didn't know that a truck can be as big as a house

© Aladdin Books Ltd 1999
Produced by
Aladdin Books Ltd
28 Percy Street
London W1P 0LD

First published in the United States in 1999 by
Copper Beech Books,
an imprint of
The Millbrook Press
2 Old New Milford Road
Brookfield, Connecticut 06804

Concept, editorial, and design by
David West Children's Books
Illustrators: Ross Watton, Jo Moore

Printed in Belgium

Library of Congress Cataloging-in-Publication Data
Petty, William.
A truck can be as big as a house : and other amazing facts about trucks / by
William Petty.
p. cm. — (I didn't know that—)
Includes index.
Summary: Explores some of the largest and most powerful trucks in the world
today, from oil tankers to dump trucks, and describes the jobs they do.
ISBN 0-7613-0913-6 (lib. bdg.). — ISBN 0-7613-0796-6 (hc)
1. Trucks—Juvenile literature. [1. Trucks.] I. Titles. II. Series.
TL230.15.P48   1999   98-55543
629.224—dc21   CIP AC

5 4 3 2 1

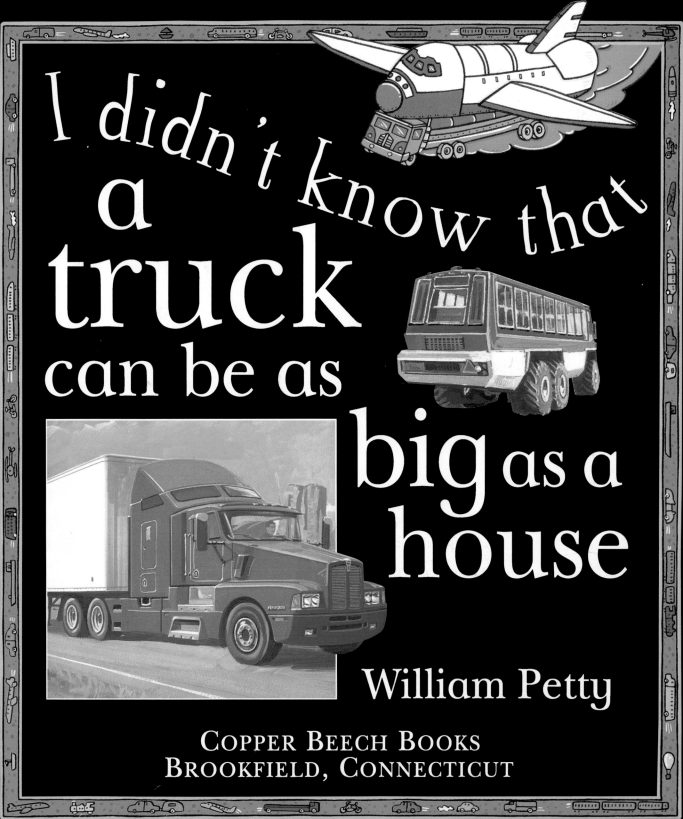

I didn't know that a truck can be as big as a house

William Petty

COPPER BEECH BOOKS
BROOKFIELD, CONNECTICUT

I didn't know that

a truck can carry a spacecraft 6

trucks used to run on steam 9

some trucks have a fifth wheel 11

a truck can be as big as a house 12

tankers can be filled with chocolate 15

some fire trucks have a driver at each end 17

a modern truck can be as comfortable as a hotel room 18

some trucks can swim 21

Juggernaut is a god 22

one truck can move eleven cars 24

modern trucks drive on air 26

you can find trucks on a race track 29

glossary 30

index 32

Introduction

Did *you* know that some trucks can be driven in water and on land? ... that the Terex Titan truck is too big to go on the road? ... that road trains can be as long as 16 cars?

Discover for yourself amazing facts about trucks. Learn about all types of trucks from the earliest steam-powered ones to today's hi-tech models.

Watch for this symbol that means there is a fun project for you to try.

Is it true or is it false? Watch for this symbol and try to answer the question before reading on for the answer.

Don't forget to check the borders for extra amazing facts.

I didn't know that

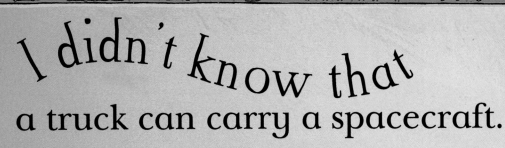

a truck can carry a spacecraft. This truck carries space shuttles to the launch site. Its enormous trailer can carry the weight of a 68-ton craft! The police have to close the roads and escort it.

 True or false?

A truck can carry a nuclear missile.

Answer: **True**

This truck is towing a nuclear missile as part of a parade. The heavy missile is not armed, but it must still be loaded very carefully.

This gas storage vessel was the longest load ever, at 275 feet long! The truck's route was planned months in advance to avoid narrow roads and tight corners. The journey took place early in the morning when the roads were less busy.

The army uses trucks like this one (below) to transport tanks over long distances by road. Tanks are ideal for crossing rough, off-road terrain, but their hard metal tracks can damage road surfaces.

7

One hundred years ago, trucks competed with horses for business. In the 1920s, Ford advertised trucks with the slogan, "It doesn't need feeding when standing still," unlike hungry horses!

True or false?
There was a truck more than 200 years ago.

Answer: **True**
In 1769 Nicolas-Joseph Cugnot built a steam tractor to pull cannons into battle (below). It went out of control during testing and was abandoned.

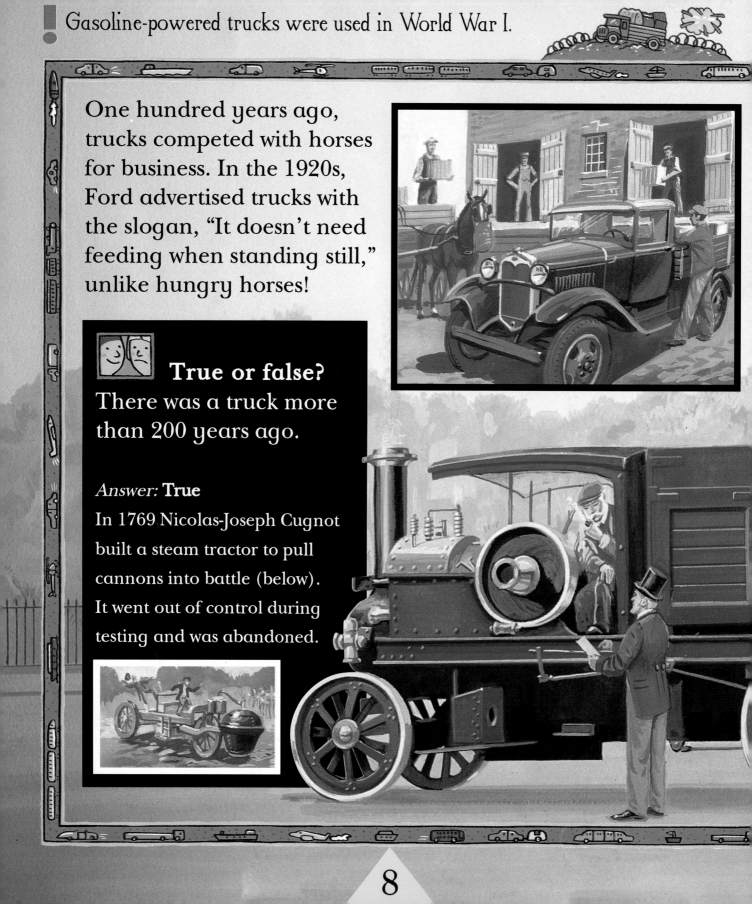

Rudolf Diesel invented the diesel engine in 1897. Today most trucks are powered by a diesel engine and *diesel fuel.*

I didn't know that

trucks used to run on steam. Before the gasoline engine became widely used, trucks were powered by steam. Water heated in a boiler became steam and turned the wheels. Today, steam is not used in trucks.

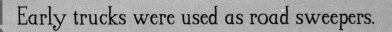
Early trucks were used as road sweepers.

Trailers are supported by "feet" when they're not attached to a cab.

True or false?
Trucks can bend.

Answer: **True**
Articulated trucks bend where the *cab* is connected to the trailer. This means that they can turn corners more easily.

Fifth wheel

Trucks can carry a lot of *cargo*. A fork-lift truck (right) is useful for loading and unloading. Its movable prongs at the front mean it can lift heavy objects onto or off a truck.

SEARCH & FIND & SEARCH & FIND &

Can you find the four wrenches?

I didn't know that

some trucks have a *fifth wheel*. The "fifth wheel" is the device that connects a tractor to its trailer. It acts like a hinge. Because the trailer can be detached, it can be easily moved from one tractor unit to another.

This funny-looking contraption was the world's first-ever *articulated* vehicle, *Thornycroft*. It was built in Britain in 1897, over 100 years ago. Although the gasoline engine had been invented by then, *Thornycroft* still ran on steam.

I didn't know that

a truck can be as big as a house. The Terex Titan has a 16-*cylinder* engine and can carry an incredible 350 tons! It is too big to travel by road and has to be assembled on-site.

SEARCH & FIND

Can you find five yellow hard hats?

FIND & SEARCH

You can see concrete mixers like this one (left) on the highway. The drum has to turn all the time, or else the wet concrete in the mixer will harden and set.

Cranes like this (right) are used on building sites to move heavy objects. The extending arm can lift things to great heights.

Atlas was a Titan, a Greek giant. He carried the world.

The tires of a Terex Titan weigh 4.5 tons each.

True or false?
Some trucks have tracks.

Answer: **True**
Some trucks are specially fitted with *Caterpillar tracks* — just like a bulldozer! They can drive over bumpy ground.

Trucks carrying dangerous substances display warning signs. They are international; no language is used. Guess what sort of dangers these four signs describe. The pictures should tell you. Try making up your own signs.

A Flammable, B Radioactive, C Explosive, D Corrosive

A

B

C

D

SEARCH & FIND Can you find the chocolate bar? FIND & SEARCH

Tankers are used to remove blockages from road drains.

Scientists are now developing *"green" fuels,* such as alcohol made from plant sap. In Brazil, the high cost of fuel led to the development of a car that runs on plant alcohol.

I didn't know that tankers can be filled with chocolate. Tankers transport all kinds of liquids. They carry fuels for cars and airplanes, as well as liquid food and drink — including liquid chocolate!

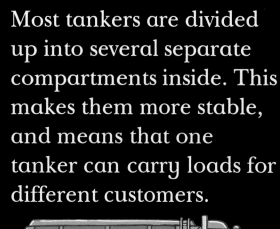

Most tankers are divided up into several separate compartments inside. This makes them more stable, and means that one tanker can carry loads for different customers.

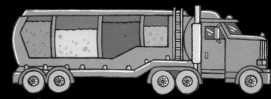

Firefighters use fire truck ladders (left) to reach the tops of buildings. The ladder can stretch to 100 feet long and can carry 1,500 pounds, even in a strong wind!

Specially designed fire trucks (right) work at airports, where a fire could be disastrous. When a plane has to make an emergency landing, they spray foam on the runway.

I didn't know that

some fire trucks have a driver at each end. The articulated Aerial Tiller fire truck has a second cab at the back. The firefighter who sits there can steer the truck through winding streets.

The Aerial Tiller's ladder carries a powerful 1,500-foot hose that delivers 1,000 gallons of water per minute. When the ladder is up, stabilizers extend out from each side to help balance the truck.

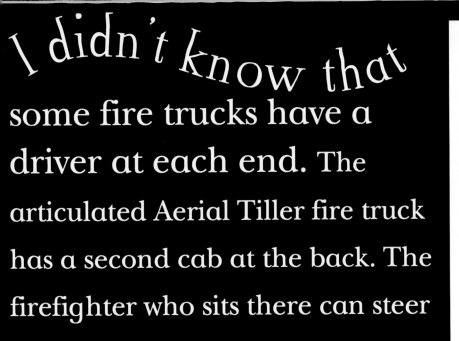

Stabilizers stop a fire truck from falling over.

I didn't know that

a modern truck can be as comfortable as a hotel room.

Can you find the suitcase?

Long-distance truck drivers who spend several weeks away from home may live in their cabs. The trucks can come with many

comforts — a bed, a TV, and even a sink!

Imagine having to find your way around all the knobs and dials in a modern truck cab like the one above! Before you can drive a big truck, you have to take a special driving test.

A modern truck cab has to contain as much as possible in a small space. Try designing a cab, including everything you would like to have with you when you are away from home.

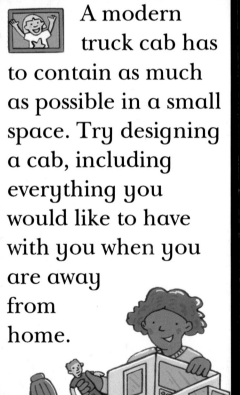

Some trucks have more than twenty gears.

CB radio

Second bunk

First bunk

Storage
space

Control
panel

Movable
passenger
seat

19

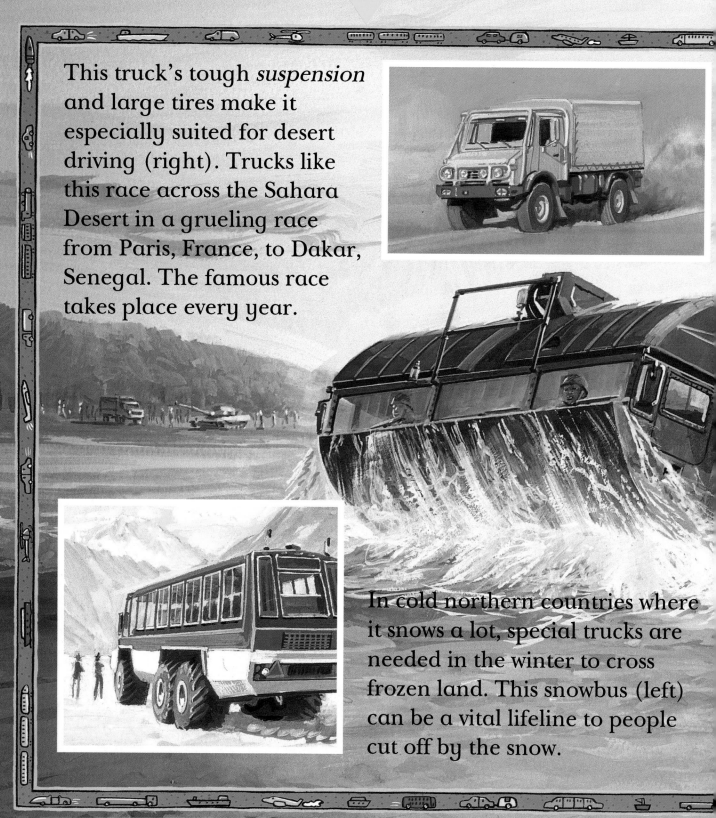

This truck's tough *suspension* and large tires make it especially suited for desert driving (right). Trucks like this race across the Sahara Desert in a grueling race from Paris, France, to Dakar, Senegal. The famous race takes place every year.

In cold northern countries where it snows a lot, special trucks are needed in the winter to cross frozen land. This snowbus (left) can be a vital lifeline to people cut off by the snow.

Truck are used as snow plows.

I didn't know that

some trucks can swim.
This army truck is *amphibious* — it can travel on land or in water. The engine turns wheels and a propeller. Its flat top means it can form a bridge to transport other vehicles over water.

Snow chains fitted to a tire like this give a truck or a car the extra grip it needs to drive across ice and snow without skidding.

I didn't know that

Juggernaut is a god. Enormous trucks are called juggernauts, after a Hindu god. In Puri, India, people used to throw themselves under the wheels of the giant cart that carried a statue of the god.

SEARCH & FIND
Can you find three teddy bears?
FIND & SEARCH

This crane is loading a *container* onto a truck. Because the containers are detachable, they can be moved from trucks to boats or trains and back easily. They can also be stored neatly.

In countries where there are few railroads, such as Australia, "road trains" like this one above carry goods over long distances. Road trains consist of four or five trailers linked together. The longest-ever road train was the length of 16 cars!

Trucks were banned from the first U.S. freeway in 1925.

I didn't know that

one truck can move eleven cars. Cars are often moved around using one of these transport trucks. Because it has two or even three layers, the transporter can carry eleven, or even more, cars at the same time.

SEARCH & FIND

Can you find the yellow headlights?

FIND & SEARCH

Trucks can also be transported. The trucks above are being loaded on to a Channel Tunnel train. It carries them under the sea between England and France at speeds of 90 miles per hour.

Articulated trucks can be transported "piggy-back" style.

Cars on a transport truck have to be loaded in a certain order. The first car sits above the cab. Next, the top level and then the bottom level are filled with cars. For unloading the cars, the sequence is reversed.

I didn't know that

modern trucks drive on air.
Today's hi-tech trucks are equipped
with *compressed air* tanks. High-pressure
air at work in the brake and suspension
systems ensures fast braking
and a smooth ride.

SEARCH & FIND
Can you find the road runner?
FIND & SEARCH

In the future, all
trucks might look
like this! They will
be made with new materials — lighter and
stronger than those of today. They will also
produce less pollution than older trucks.

Fuel tank

Some trucks have as many as 22 wheels.

Modern trucks have artificial grass on wheel arches to catch spray.

This truck (left) is being tested in a *wind tunnel* to find out how aerodynamic it is — how easily it cuts through the air. A sleek, streamlined truck requires less power to move it forward.

Aerodynamic driver's quarters

Driver's cab

True or false?

Some truck cabs flip up.

Answer: **True**

Some truck cabs flip up so mechanics can check the engine underneath. Trucks that flip like this are called cab-over units.

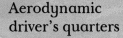

A truck powered by three jet engines reached 375 mph.

Have you ever seen a truck like this one (left)? "Monster trucks" are normal trucks but with huge wheels, powerful engines, and strong suspension. They are big enough to crush ordinary cars under their tires! Watch for monster truck shows near you!

This truck (above) has been customized. It has been given a special paint job, and some parts have been replaced. This means the truck is unique — each one is different!

I didn't know that

you can find trucks on a race track. Skilled drivers race trucks in competitions. They give them extra-powerful engines — great for high-speed driving! Racing trucks are made of lightweight materials.

True or false?

Trucks can do stunts.

Answer: **True**

This truck is doing a wheelie. It has to have a lot of power in its back wheels to do this.

Some monster trucks can weigh more than 10 tons.

Glossary

Amphibious truck

A land truck that can also swim. Its engine drives both the wheels and a propeller.

Articulated truck

A truck built in two sections so the front can bend at an angle to the back to help it turn corners.

Cab

The front part of a truck, where the driver sits.

Cargo

The load carried by a truck.

Caterpillar tracks

Wide belts made of metal or rubber plates, driven by cogs, that are used instead of wheels on some heavy vehicles.

Compressed air

Air squashed into a small space. Compressed air expands if it is allowed to, so it can push parts of a machine.

Container

A big box, usually made of steel, for carrying a cargo. It can be loaded onto a truck, a train, or a ship.

Cylinder

A hollow tube inside an engine in which gas expands to push a piston up and down.

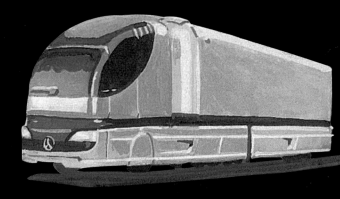

Diesel fuel

The most common type of truck fuel. It is also used to power ships, buses, and some trains and cars.

Fifth wheel

The linkage that connects an articulated truck's tractor to its trailer.

"Green" fuel

A fuel that gives off less harmful gases. Green fuels, like seaweed, are renewable — they can be grown or produced. They should not, therefore, run out.

Suspension

A system of springs or other devices that smooth out the ride in a vehicle.

Wind tunnel

A machine that blows air over a vehicle. Using computers, it then shows scientists how the air flows over the surfaces.

Index

aerodynamic 27
airplane 15
airport 16
amphibious 21, 30
army 7, 21
articulated 10, 11, 17, 24, 30, 31

brakes 26

cab 10, 18, 25, 27, 30, 31
cargo 10, 30
Caterpillar tracks 13, 30
compressed air 26, 30
concrete mixer 12
container 23, 30
cranes 12
Cugnot, Nicolas-Joseph 8
customized 29
cylinder 12, 31

diesel fuel 9, 31
Diesel, Rudolf 9

engines 9, 12, 27, 28, 29, 30

fifth wheel 10, 11, 31
fire truck 16-17
forklift truck 10

gasoline 8, 9, 11
"green" fuels 15, 31

Juggernaut 22

monster trucks 28

nuclear missiles 6

Paris-Dakar Rally 20, 21

roads 6-7, 12, 23
road trains 23

Sahara Desert 20
snow chains 21
space shuttle 6
steam 9, 11
stunts 29
suspension 20, 26, 28, 31

tankers 14, 15
tanks 7
Terex Titan 12, 13
trailers 6, 10, 11, 23, 31
transport trucks 24-25

wheels 9, 21, 26, 28, 30
wind tunnel 27, 31

Titles available in the series:
I Didn't Know That

The **sun** is a star
You can jump higher on the **moon**
Some **snakes** spit poison
Some **bugs** glow in the dark
Spiders have fangs
Some **birds** hang upside down
Dinosaurs laid eggs
Some **trains** run on water
Some **planes** hover
Some **plants** grow in midair
Sharks keep losing their teeth
People chase **twisters**
Mountains gush lava and ash
Some **boats** have wings
Whales can sing
Crocodiles yawn to keep cool
Chimps use tools
Only some **big cats** can roar
A **truck** can be as big as a house
Quakes split the ground open